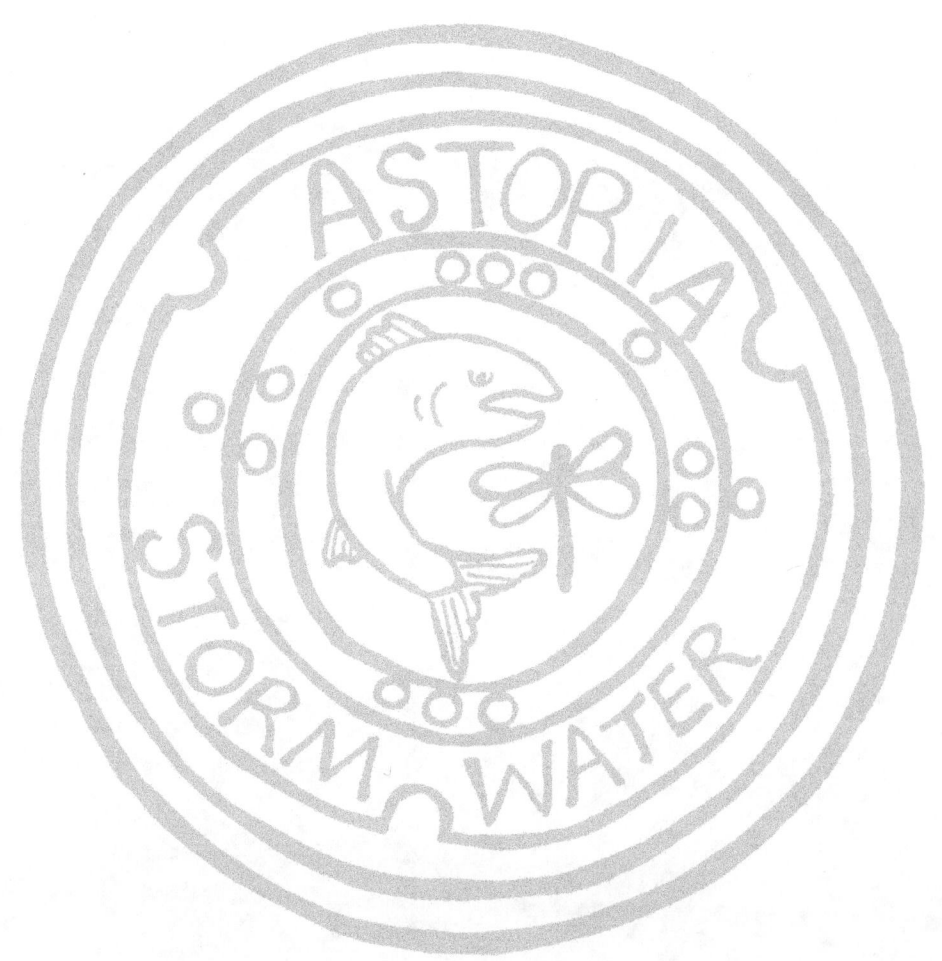

My Astoria East to West Coloring Book
© 2016 Heather Douglas
Astoria, Oregon

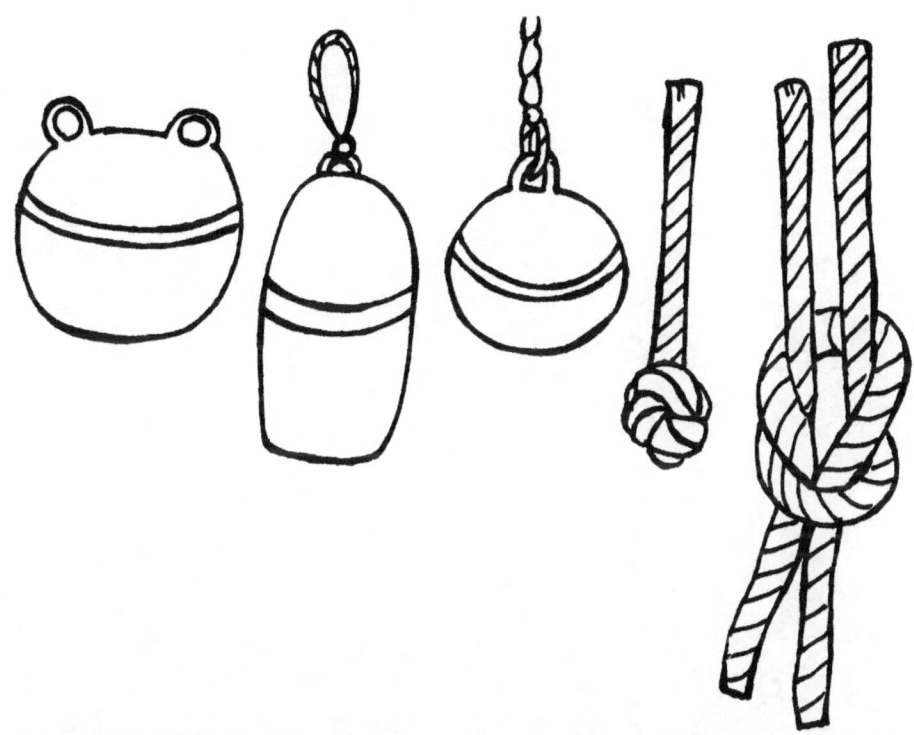

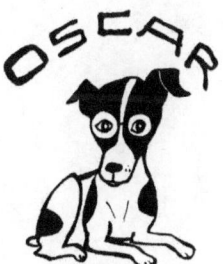

OSCAR

Oscar Astoria

oscarastoria.com
facebook.com/oscarastoria/

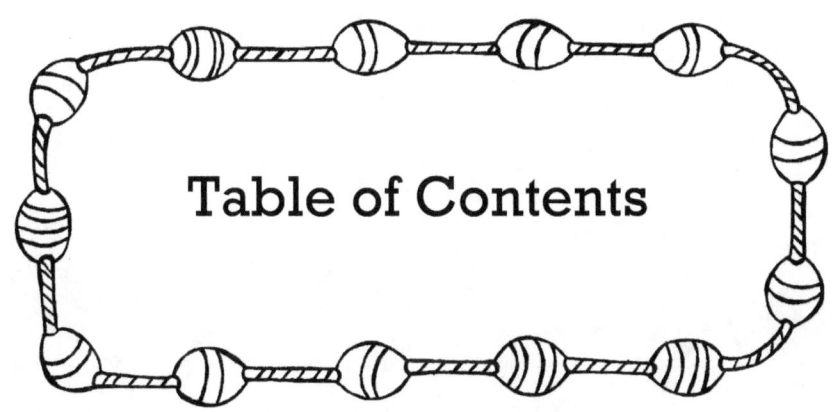

Table of Contents

A Note From the Author

I was born and raised in Astoria, Oregon. A lot has changed, and it doesn't seem to be slowing down anytime soon.

It started with a single drawing of The Custard King in 2015. Returning from three years overseas, the iconic building (which was for sale before I left the country) had since been purchased and was scheduled to shed its old pink and purple paint job for a stately blue and gold update.

Before the burger joint of my childhood was gone forever, my instinct was to sketch; strange, considering I had put aside my passion for art decades ago to pursue more practical things in life.

Luckily, passion wins out eventually. ;)

The sketches were almost entirely created with Micron Pens, copy paper and a light table. The art and the ideas for the book were jotted down on scraps of paper often shoved into my purse, because ideas exist on their own timeline.

In the world of digital perfection, my own eye gravitates towards hand drawn art— the wobbly bits, the imperfections, uneven lines.

Over time I had enough for a book.

In the end, the hardest part was deciding what to include.
Most of the places that made it into this book
were either important to me, were iconic Astoria,
or just seemed to make a good coloring page.

There were many places I left out.

Perhaps another time, another book . . .

This book is dedicated to the brief voyage of The Fake Orca and for anyone who has ever had a crazy idea, but did it anyway.

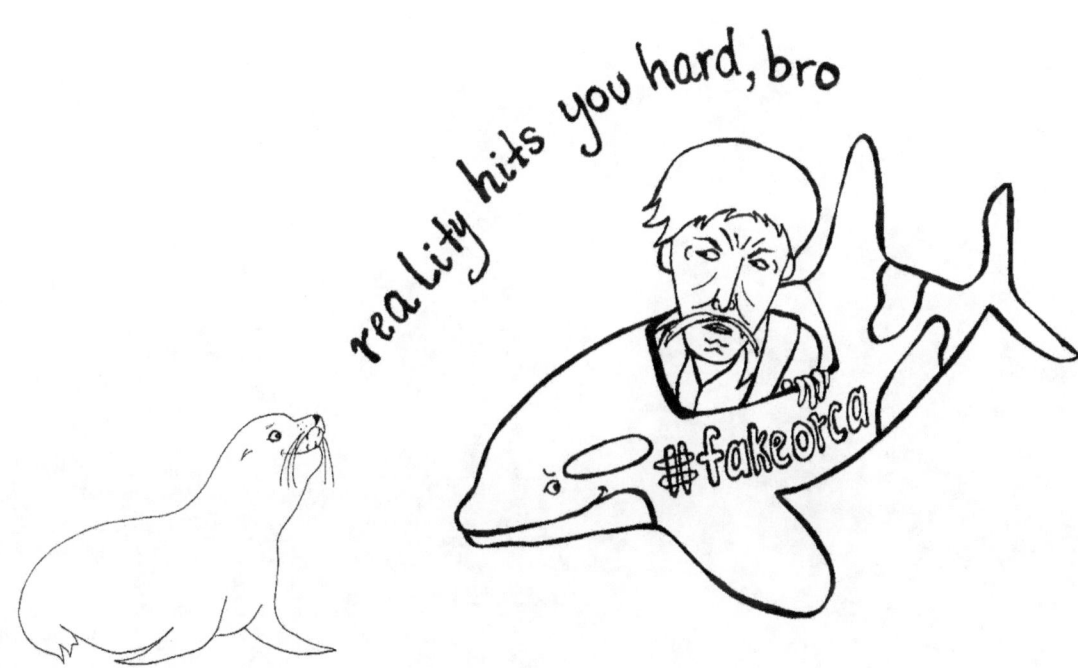

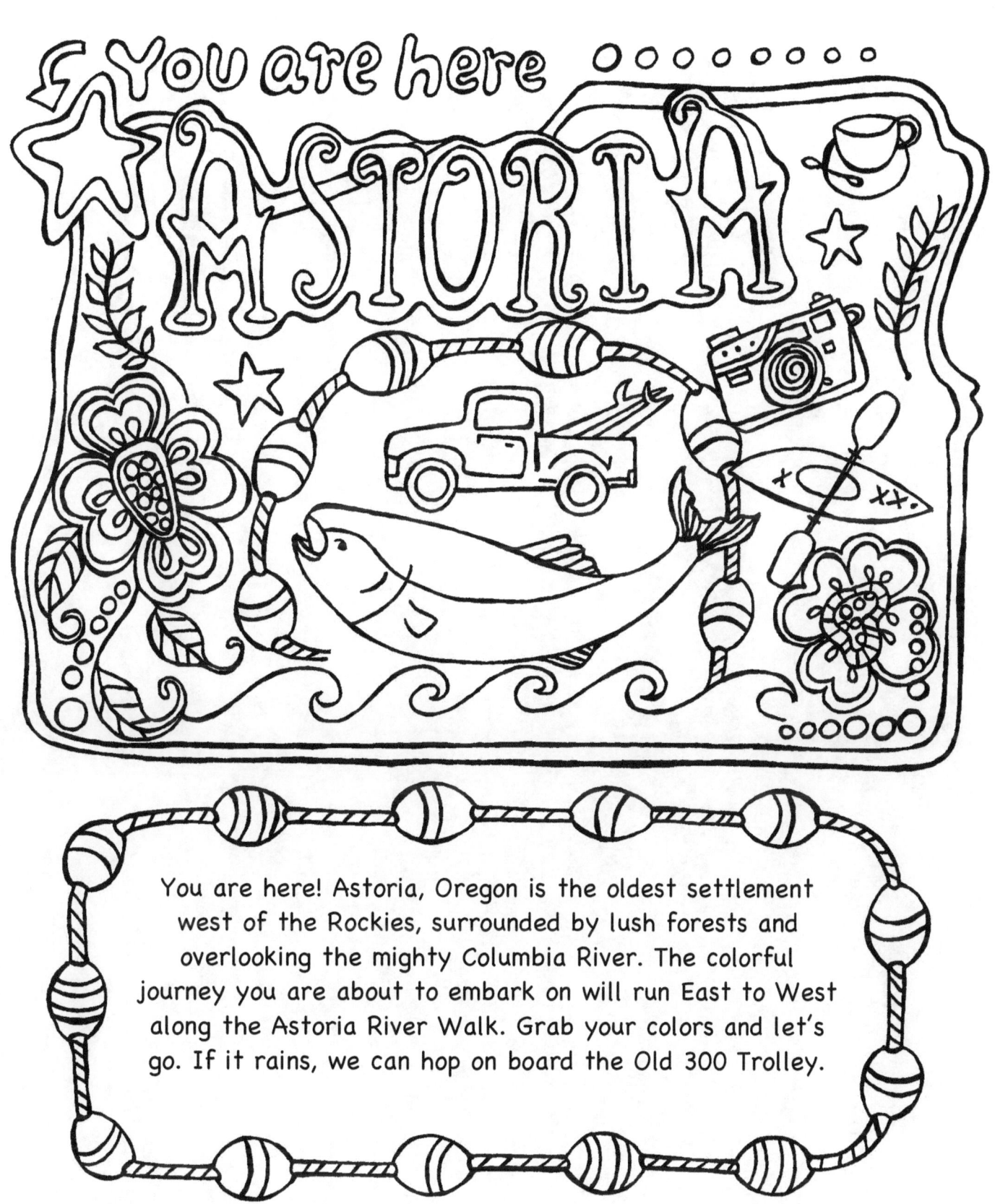

You are here! Astoria, Oregon is the oldest settlement west of the Rockies, surrounded by lush forests and overlooking the mighty Columbia River. The colorful journey you are about to embark on will run East to West along the Astoria River Walk. Grab your colors and let's go. If it rains, we can hop on board the Old 300 Trolley.

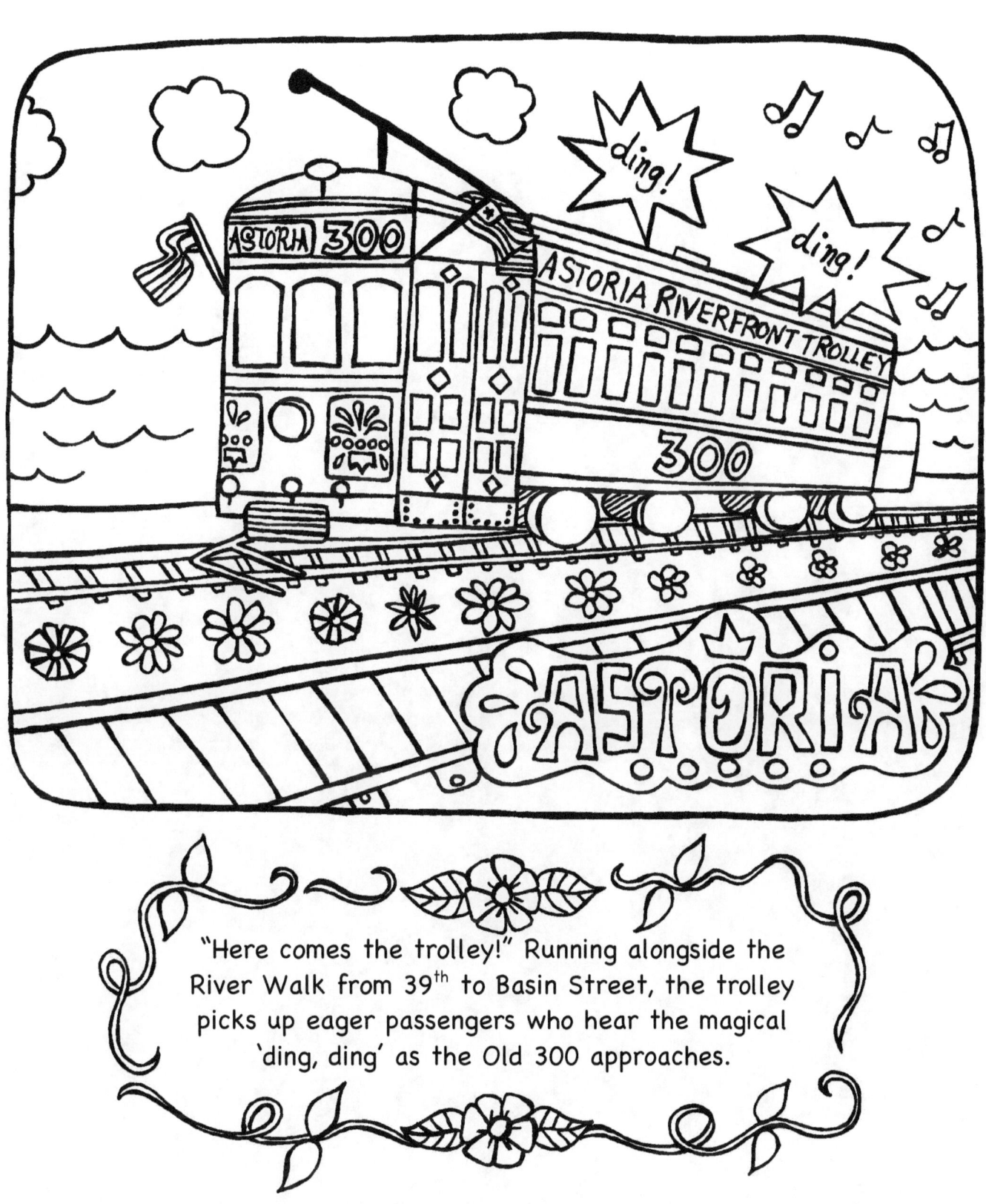

"Here comes the trolley!" Running alongside the River Walk from 39th to Basin Street, the trolley picks up eager passengers who hear the magical 'ding, ding' as the Old 300 approaches.

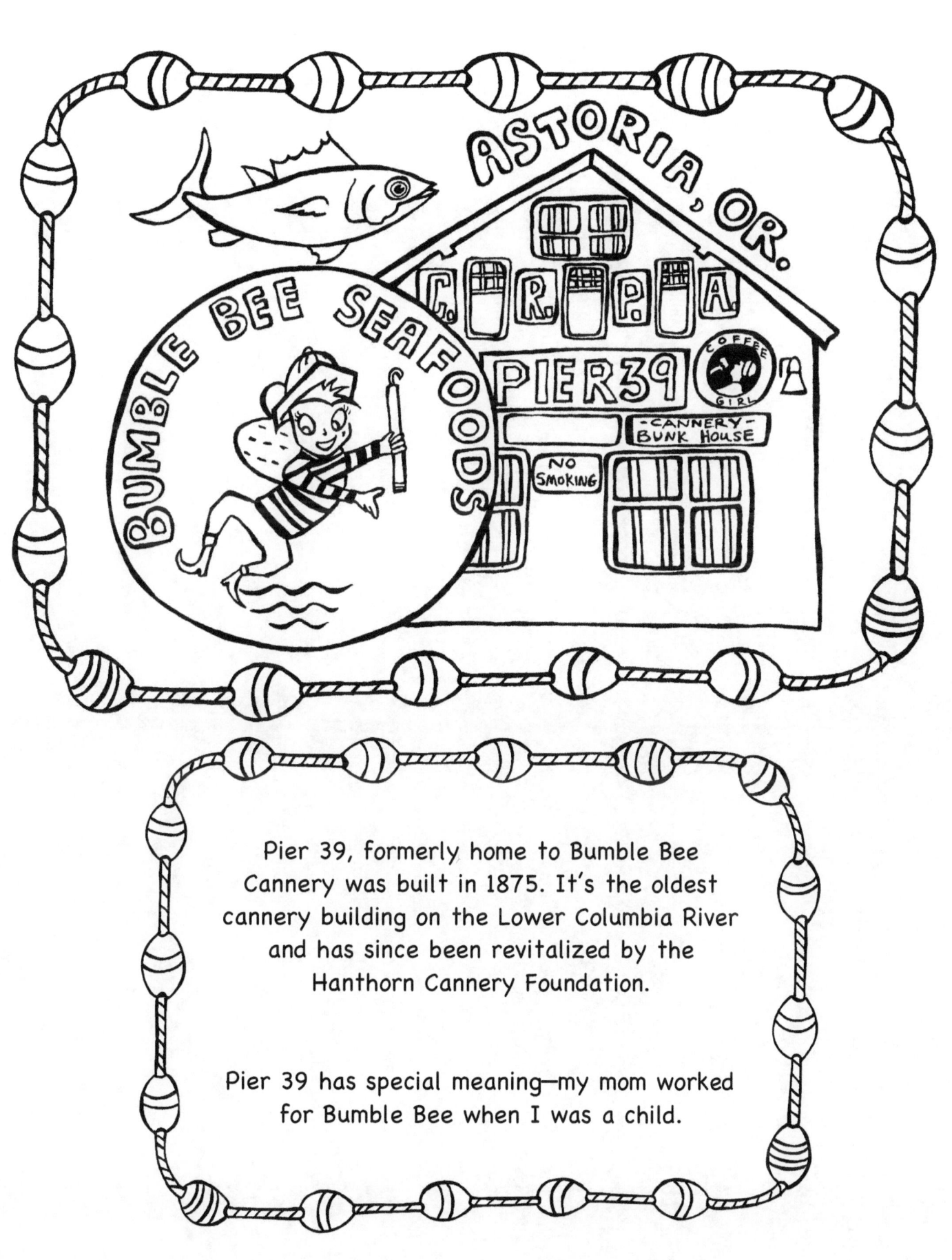

Pier 39, formerly home to Bumble Bee
Cannery was built in 1875. It's the oldest
cannery building on the Lower Columbia River
and has since been revitalized by the
Hanthorn Cannery Foundation.

Pier 39 has special meaning—my mom worked
for Bumble Bee when I was a child.

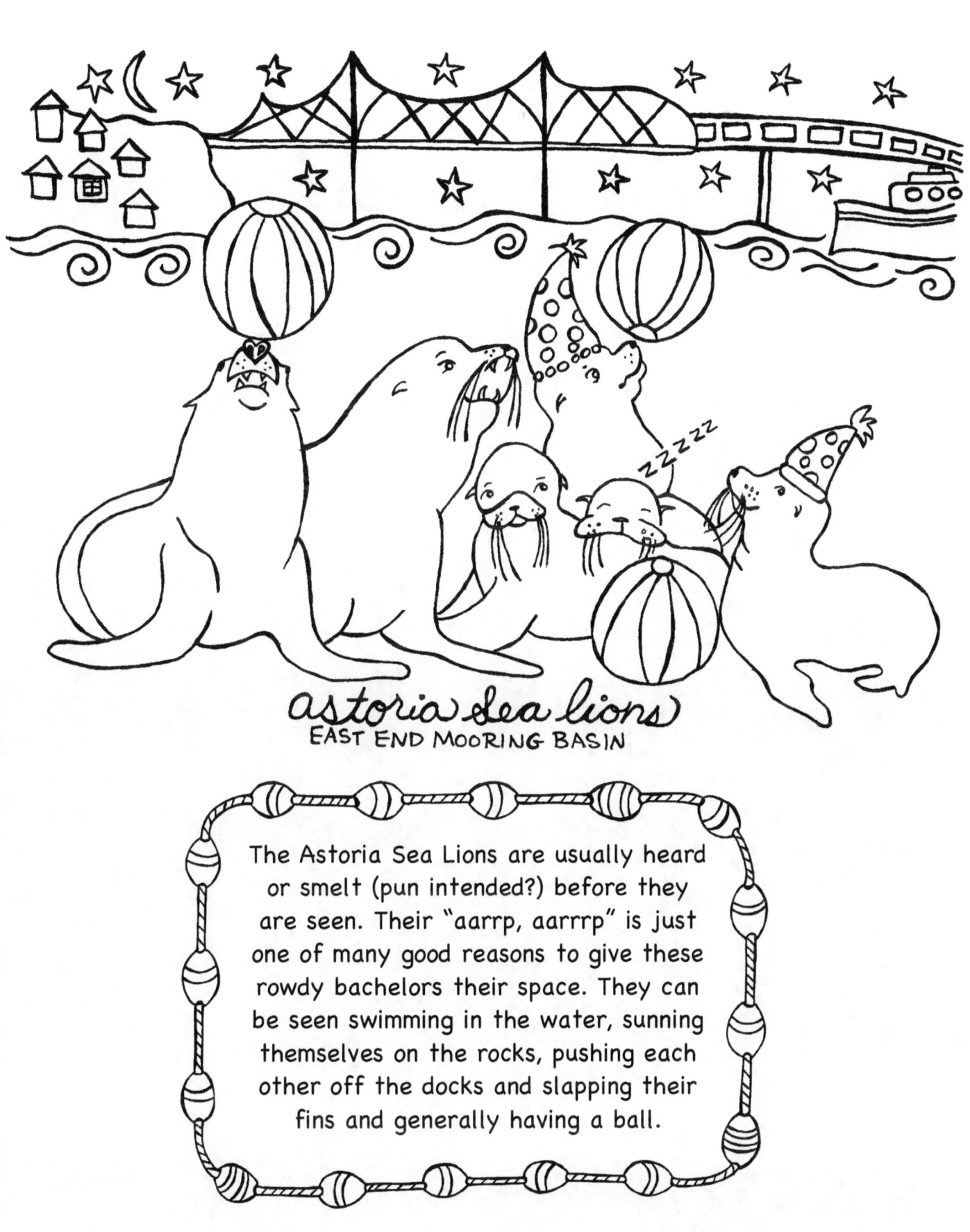

astoria sea lions
EAST END MOORING BASIN

The Astoria Sea Lions are usually heard
or smelt (pun intended?) before they
are seen. Their "aarrp, aarrrp" is just
one of many good reasons to give these
rowdy bachelors their space. They can
be seen swimming in the water, sunning
themselves on the rocks, pushing each
other off the docks and slapping their
fins and generally having a ball.

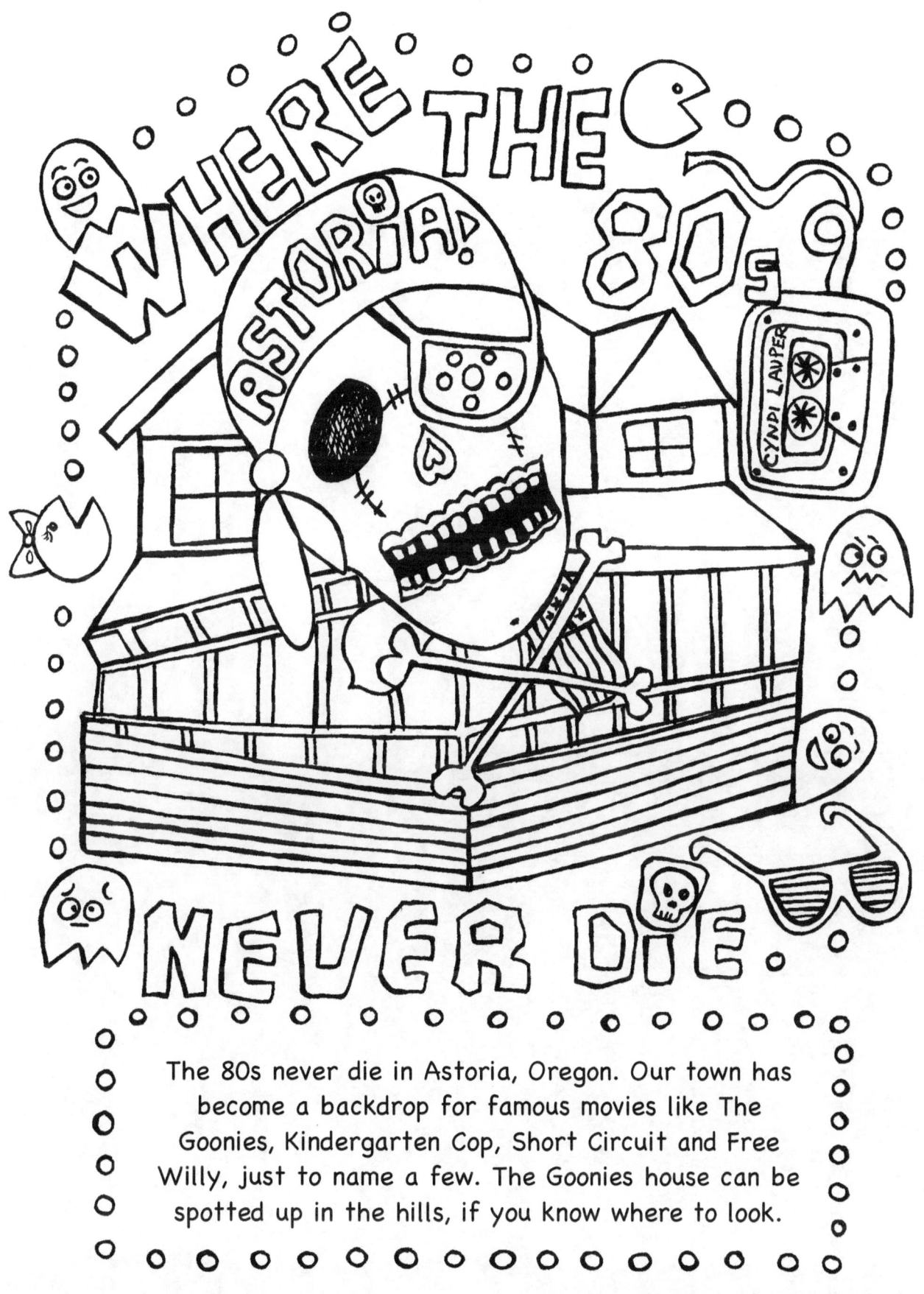

The 80s never die in Astoria, Oregon. Our town has become a backdrop for famous movies like The Goonies, Kindergarten Cop, Short Circuit and Free Willy, just to name a few. The Goonies house can be spotted up in the hills, if you know where to look.

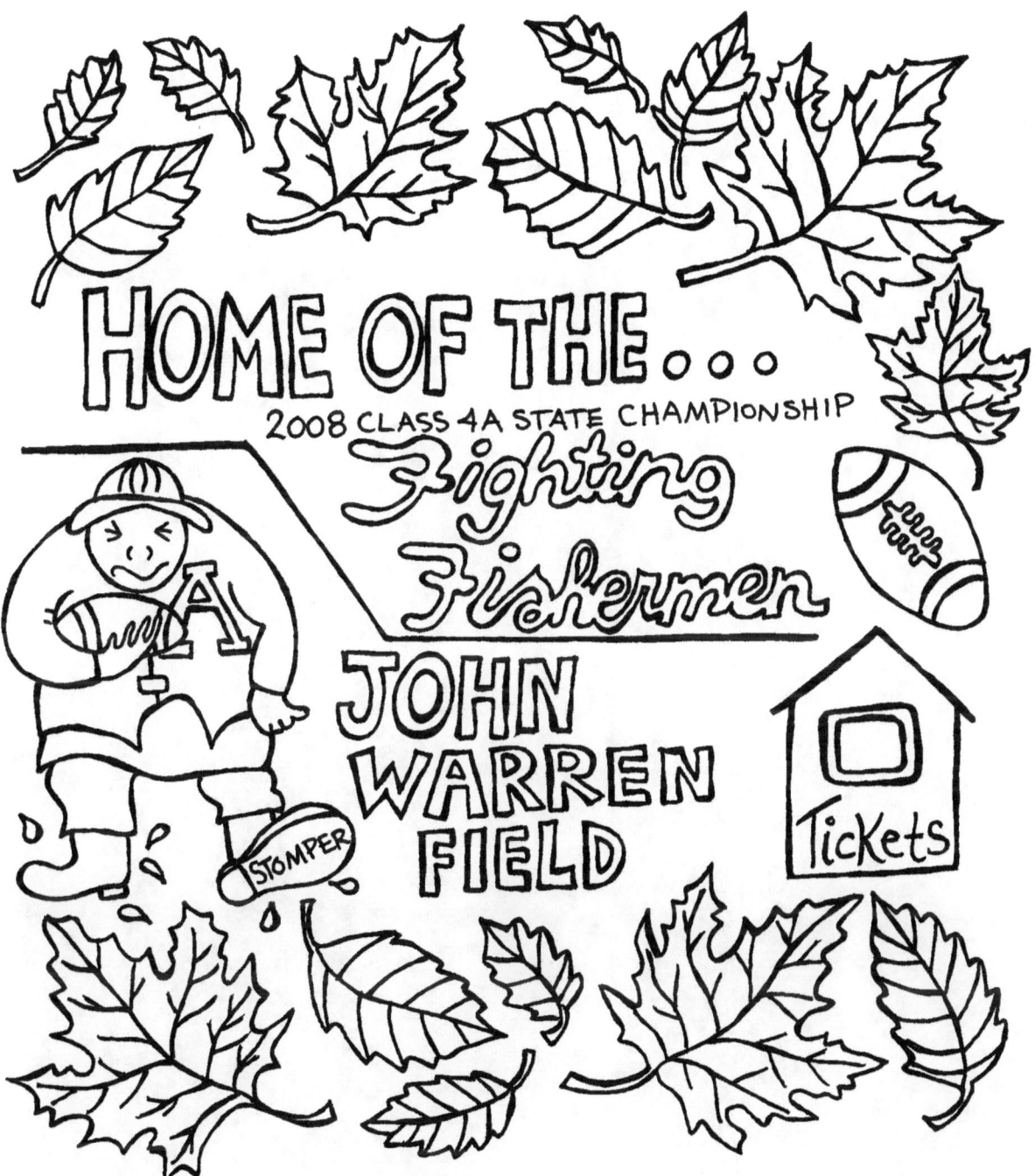

Locals and Goonie lovers alike said one last goodbye to The John Warren Field during the 30 Year Anniversary Goonies Celebration in 2015. The location is just one example of how fast Astoria is changing. The iconic purple and gold structure with the oafish Fighting Fisherman was demolished hours after this drawing was completed.

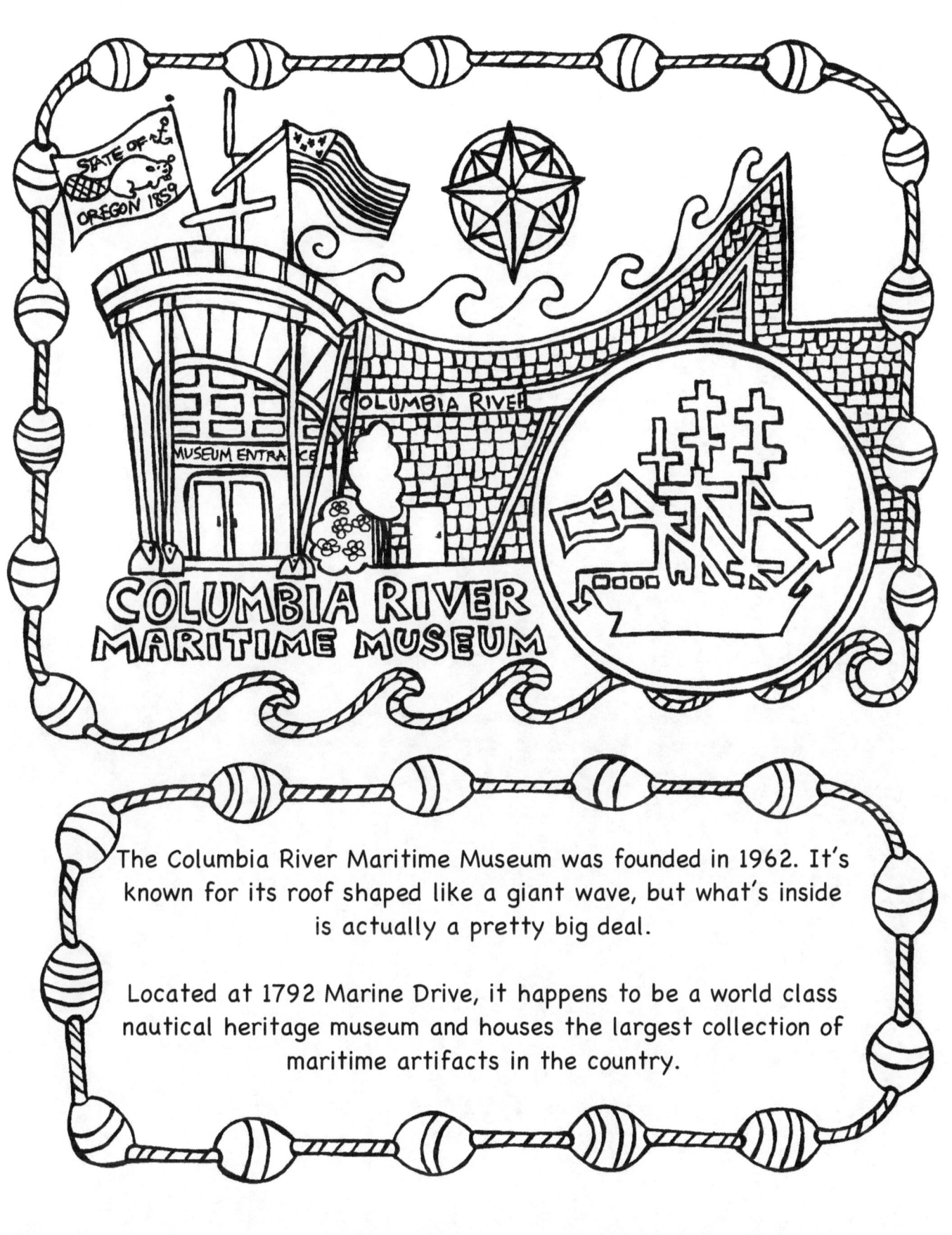

COLUMBIA RIVER
MARITIME MUSEUM

The Columbia River Maritime Museum was founded in 1962. It's known for its roof shaped like a giant wave, but what's inside is actually a pretty big deal.

Located at 1792 Marine Drive, it happens to be a world class nautical heritage museum and houses the largest collection of maritime artifacts in the country.

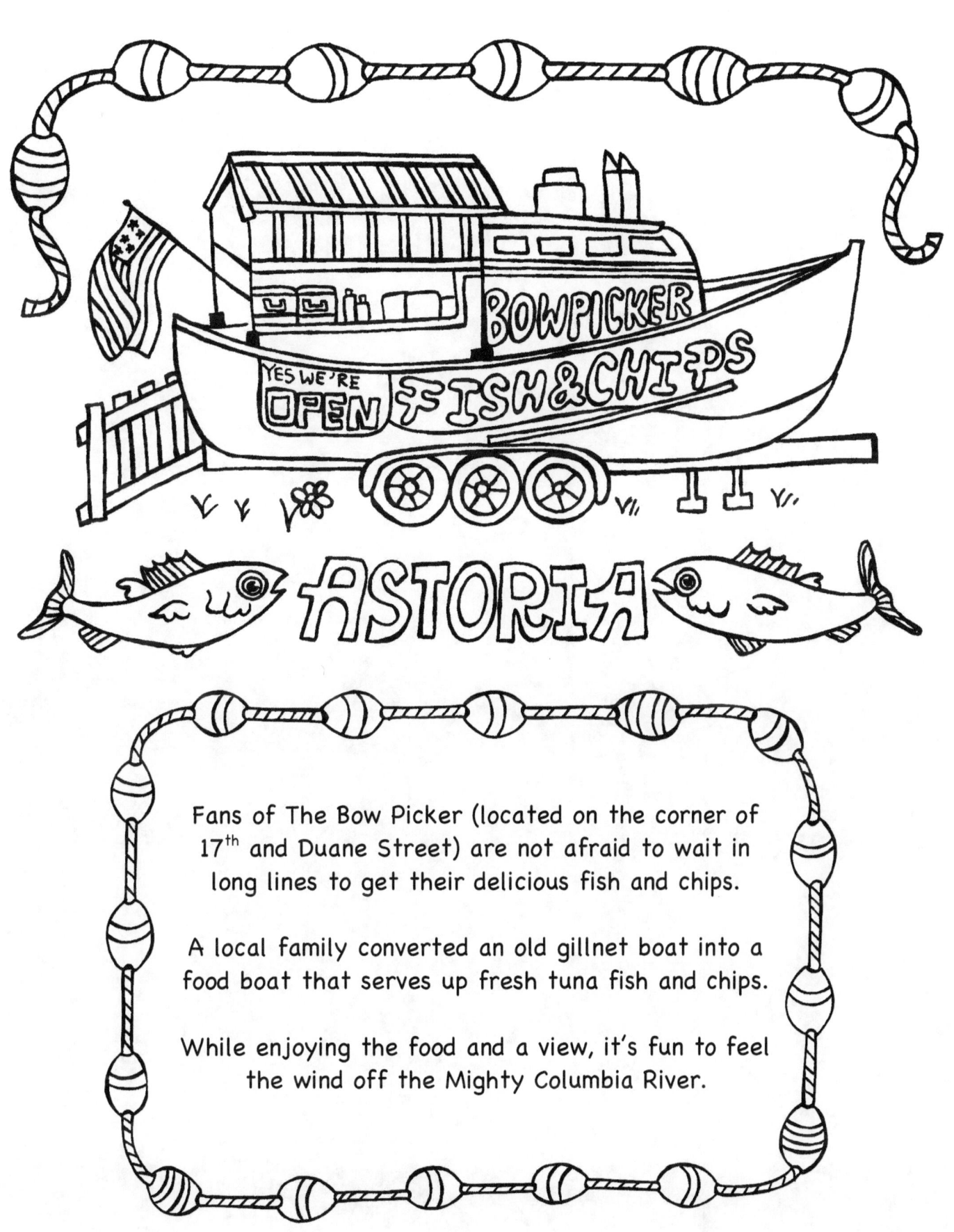

BOWPICKER

YES WE'RE OPEN FISH&CHIPS

ASTORIA

Fans of The Bow Picker (located on the corner of 17th and Duane Street) are not afraid to wait in long lines to get their delicious fish and chips.

A local family converted an old gillnet boat into a food boat that serves up fresh tuna fish and chips.

While enjoying the food and a view, it's fun to feel the wind off the Mighty Columbia River.

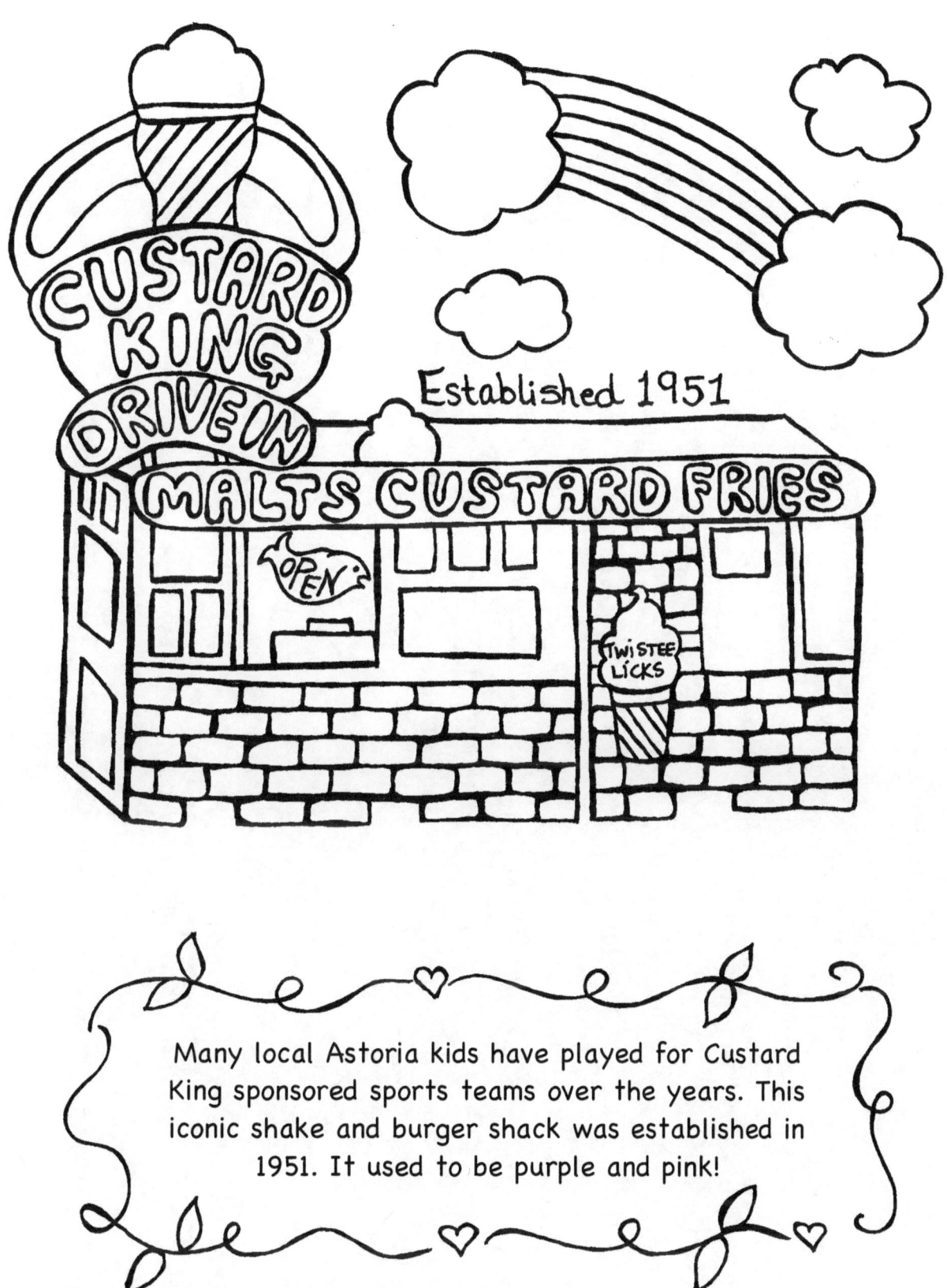

Established 1951

Many local Astoria kids have played for Custard King sponsored sports teams over the years. This iconic shake and burger shack was established in 1951. It used to be purple and pink!

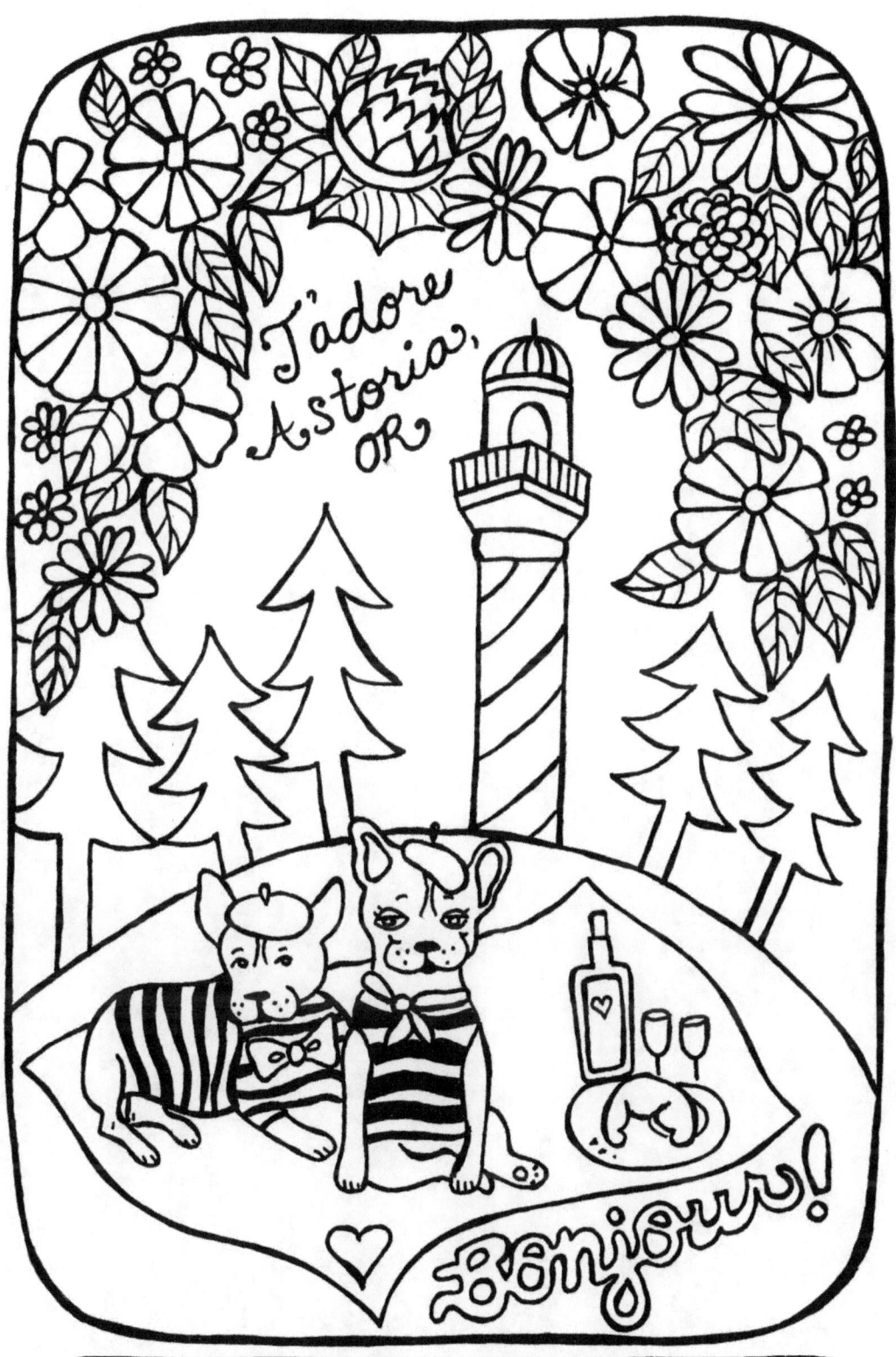

Venturing off the River Walk and up 16th Street
will require a bit of a detour, but I promise the
view will be worth it. Atop Coxcomb Hill sits the
Astoria Column—take 164 steps to the top, or
enjoy a picnic on the hill at the column's base.

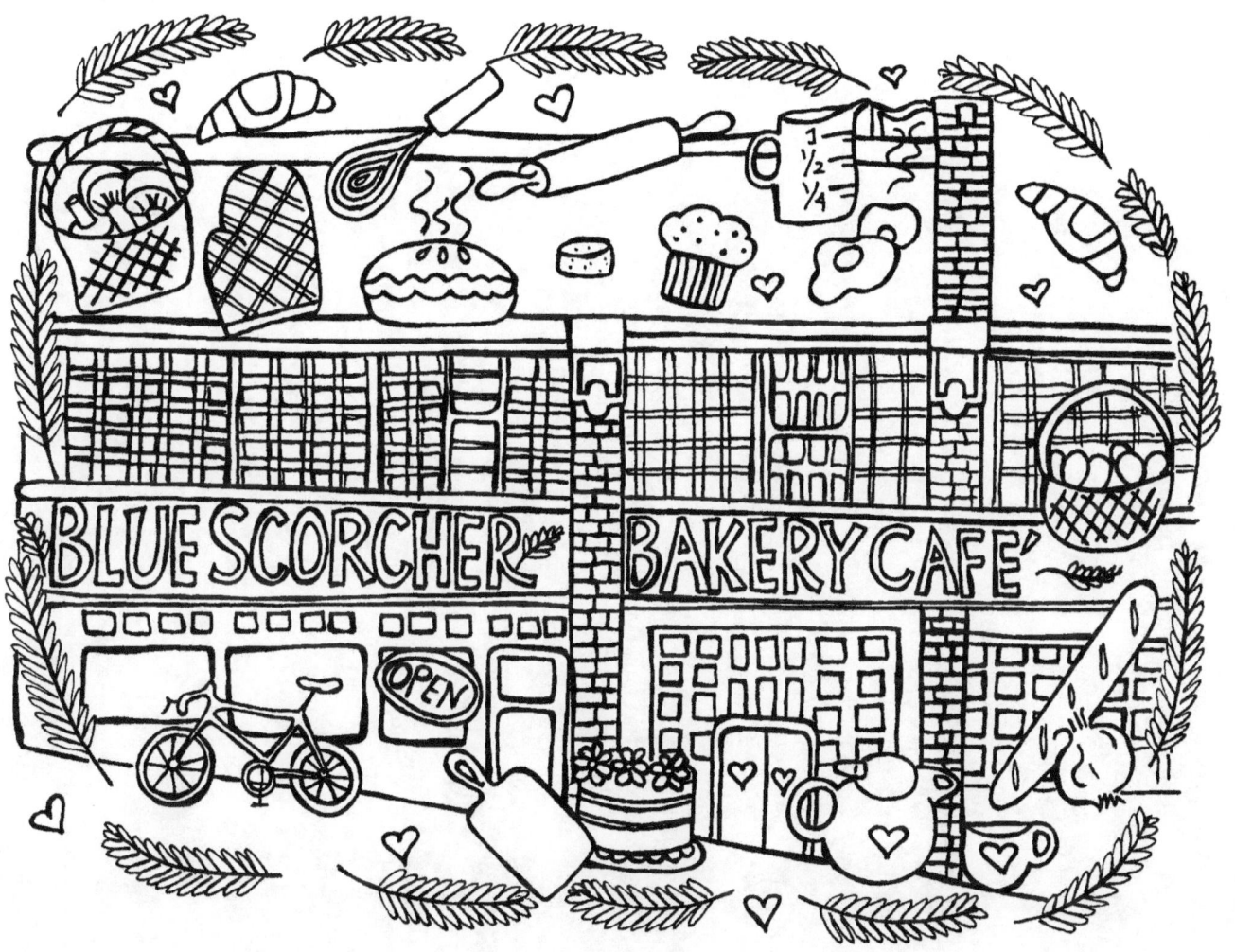

Heading back down 16th Street from the Astoria Column
to the corner of 15th and Duane, you will find
The Blue Scorcher Bakery and Café.

The 'Scorcher' is named after a fast bike!

The Blue Scorcher Bakery and Café is worker owned and
serves up vegetarian fare and gourmet treats with a
view of the Columbia River.

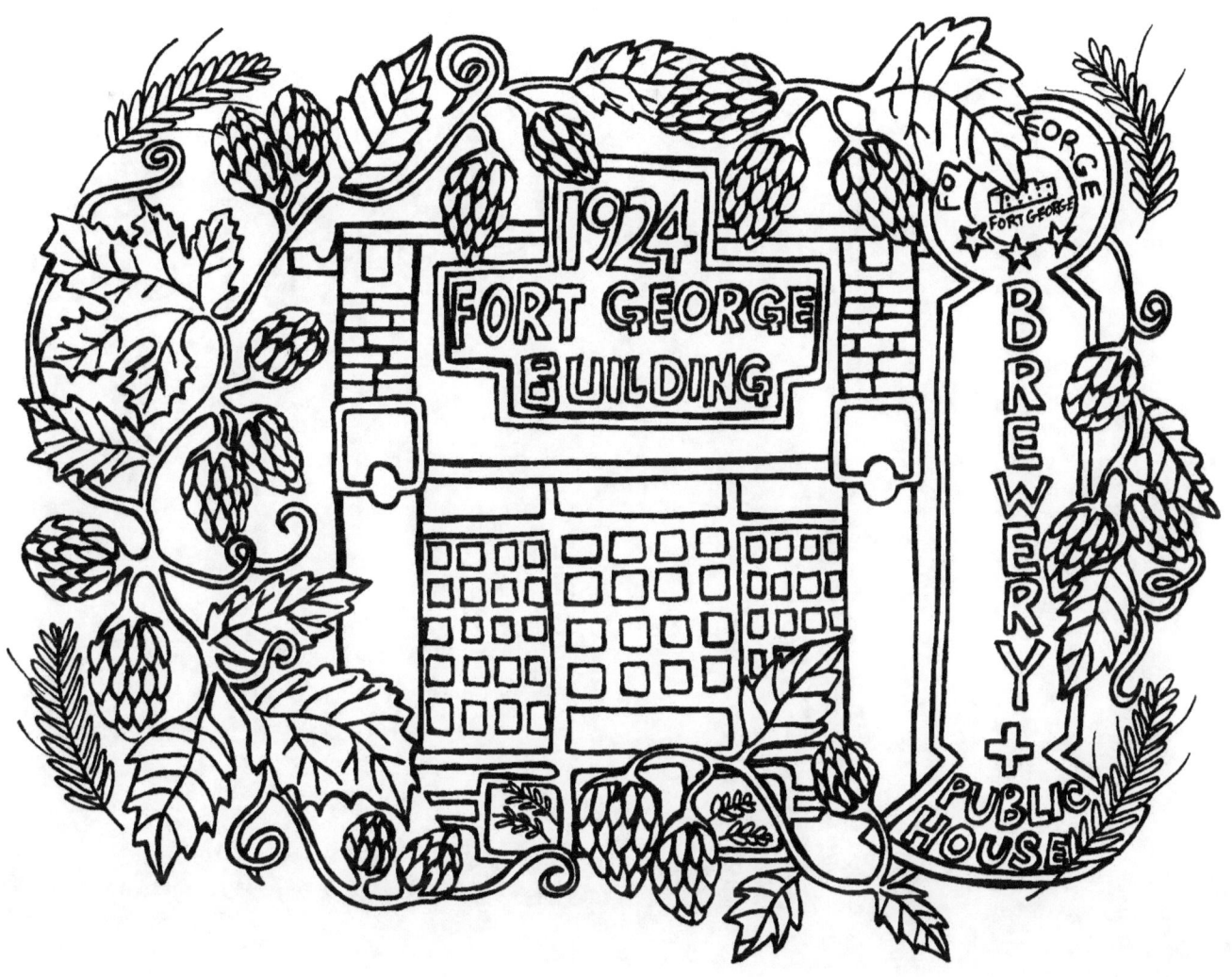

The Fort George Brewery and Public House (next door to the Blue Scorcher Bakery and Café) is situated in the revitalized Lovell Auto Building.

The popular brewery serves food as well as music on Sunday nights and hosts a number of unique events such as the annual Festival of Dark Arts each February.

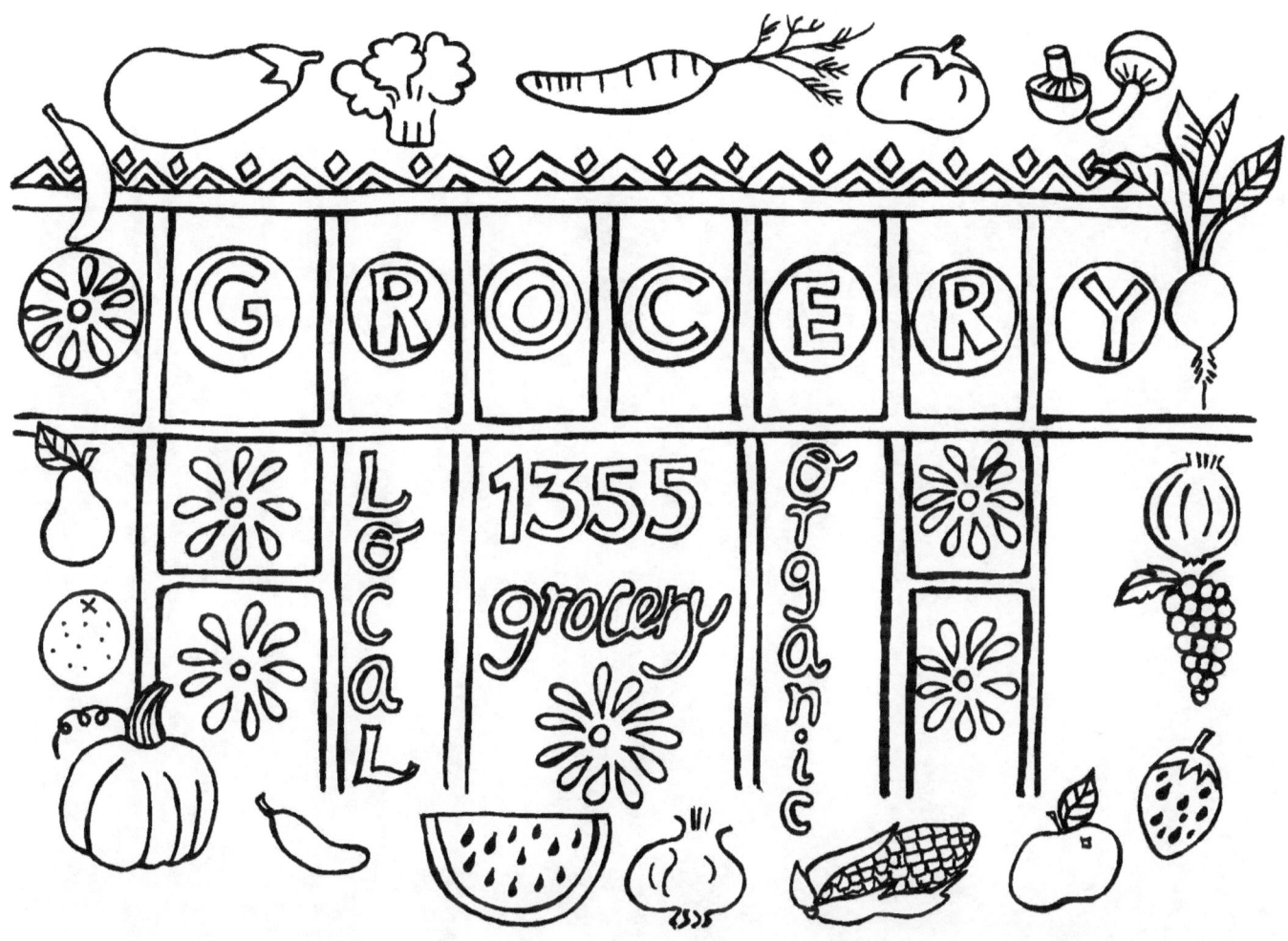

The Astoria Co-op Grocery at 1355 Exchange Street
used to be known as The Community Store.
Its beginnings trace back to the 70s.

Evolving through the years, the Astoria Co-op has
been the go-to place for organic foods along with our
local farmers markets in town.

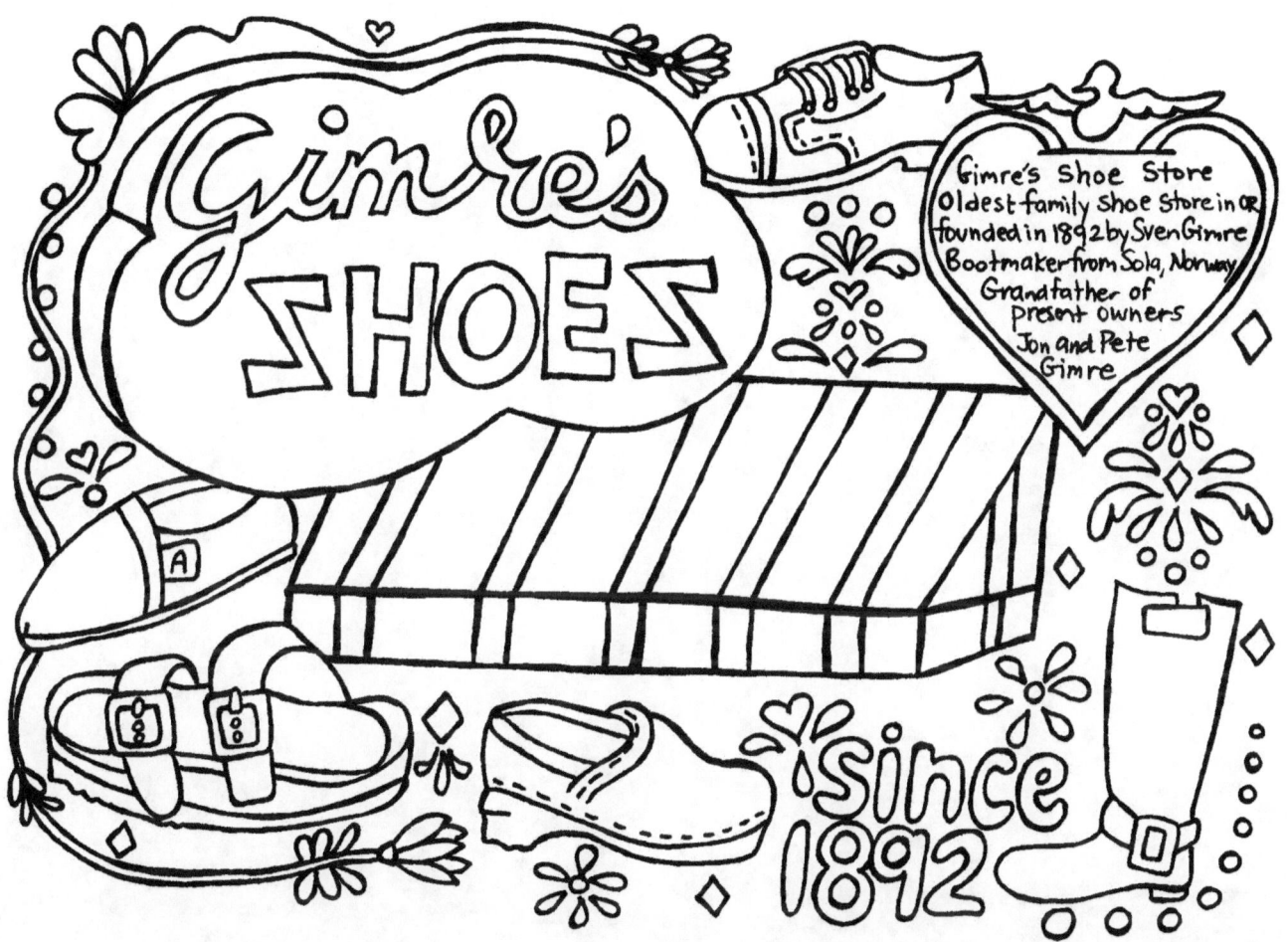

Gimre's Shoe Store
Oldest family shoe store in OR
founded in 1892 by Sven Gimre
Bootmaker from Sola, Norway.
Grandfather of
present owners
Jon and Pete
Gimre

Gimre's Shoe Store in Astoria is the oldest family shoe store in Oregon. At 239 14th Street, it's a multi-generational business with great customer service and one of the coolest vintage signs in Astoria. You can't miss the iconic green and white awning.

I still remember buying my ballet slippers at Gimre's and going to ballet class above the Liberty Theatre.

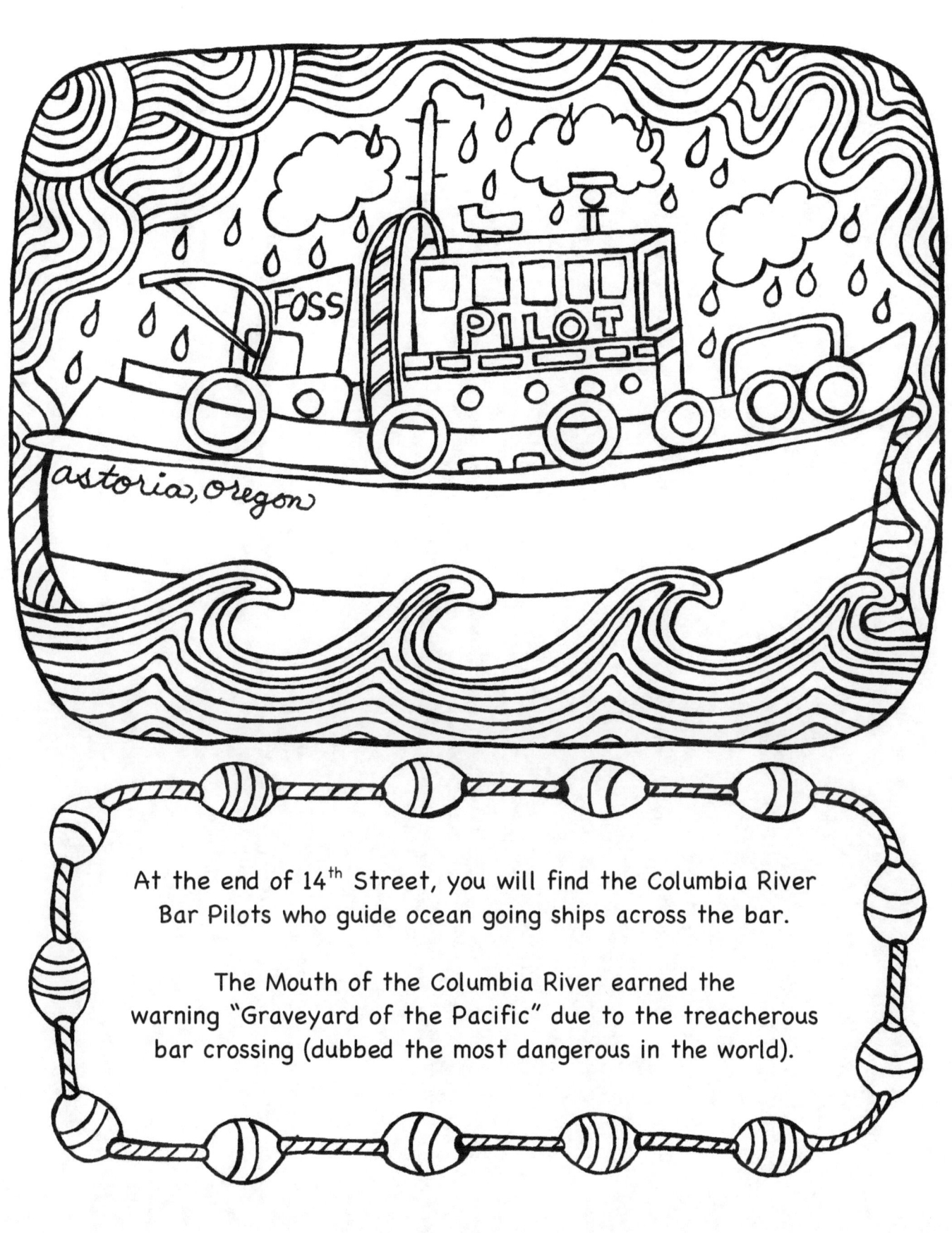

At the end of 14th Street, you will find the Columbia River
Bar Pilots who guide ocean going ships across the bar.

The Mouth of the Columbia River earned the
warning "Graveyard of the Pacific" due to the treacherous
bar crossing (dubbed the most dangerous in the world).

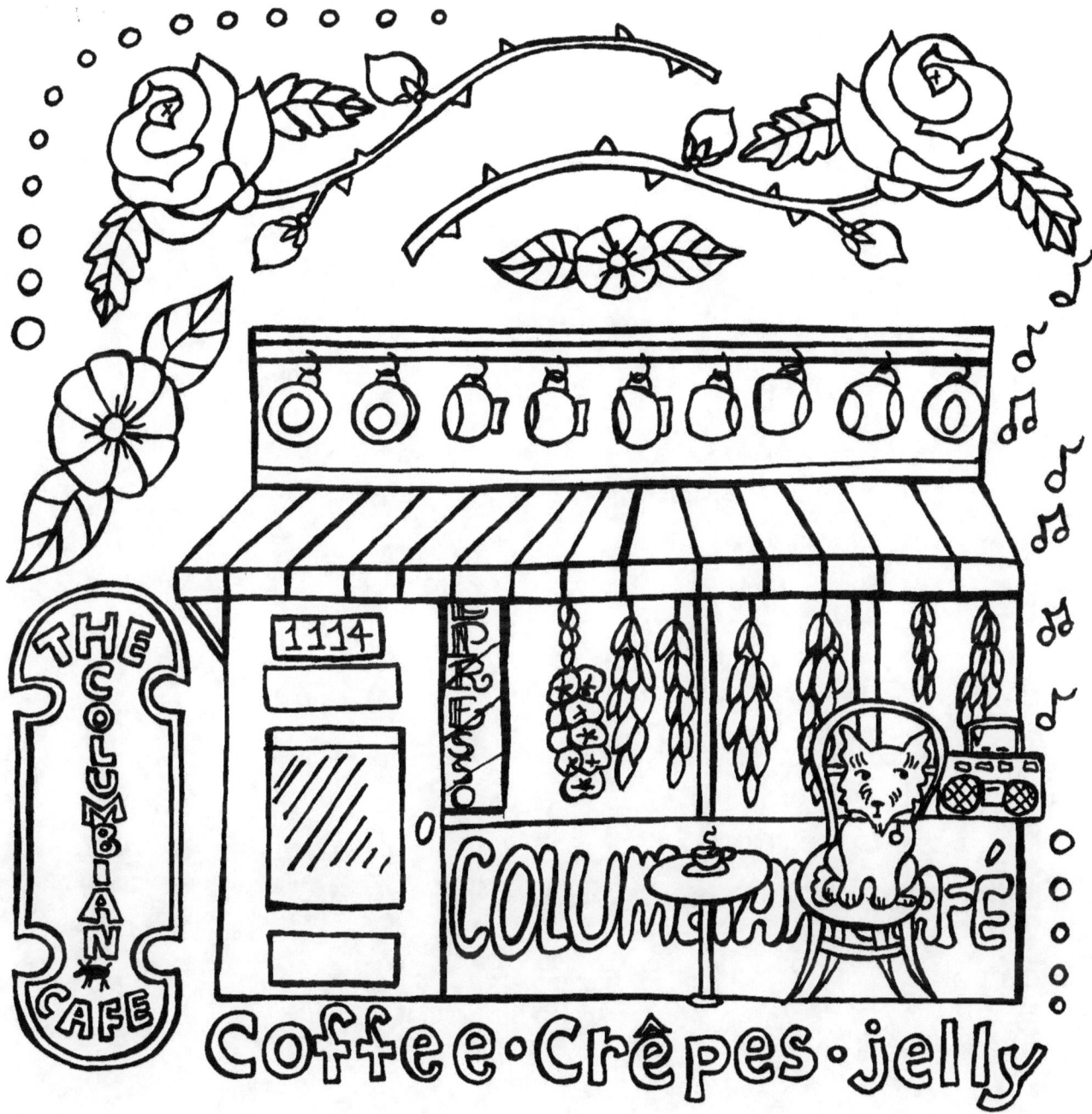

The Columbian Café, at 1114 Marine Drive with its recognizable red and white awnings is home to a very unique little café that has withstood the test of time.

Next door is the Columbian Theatre—a favorite place to eat pizza and catch an inexpensive movie.

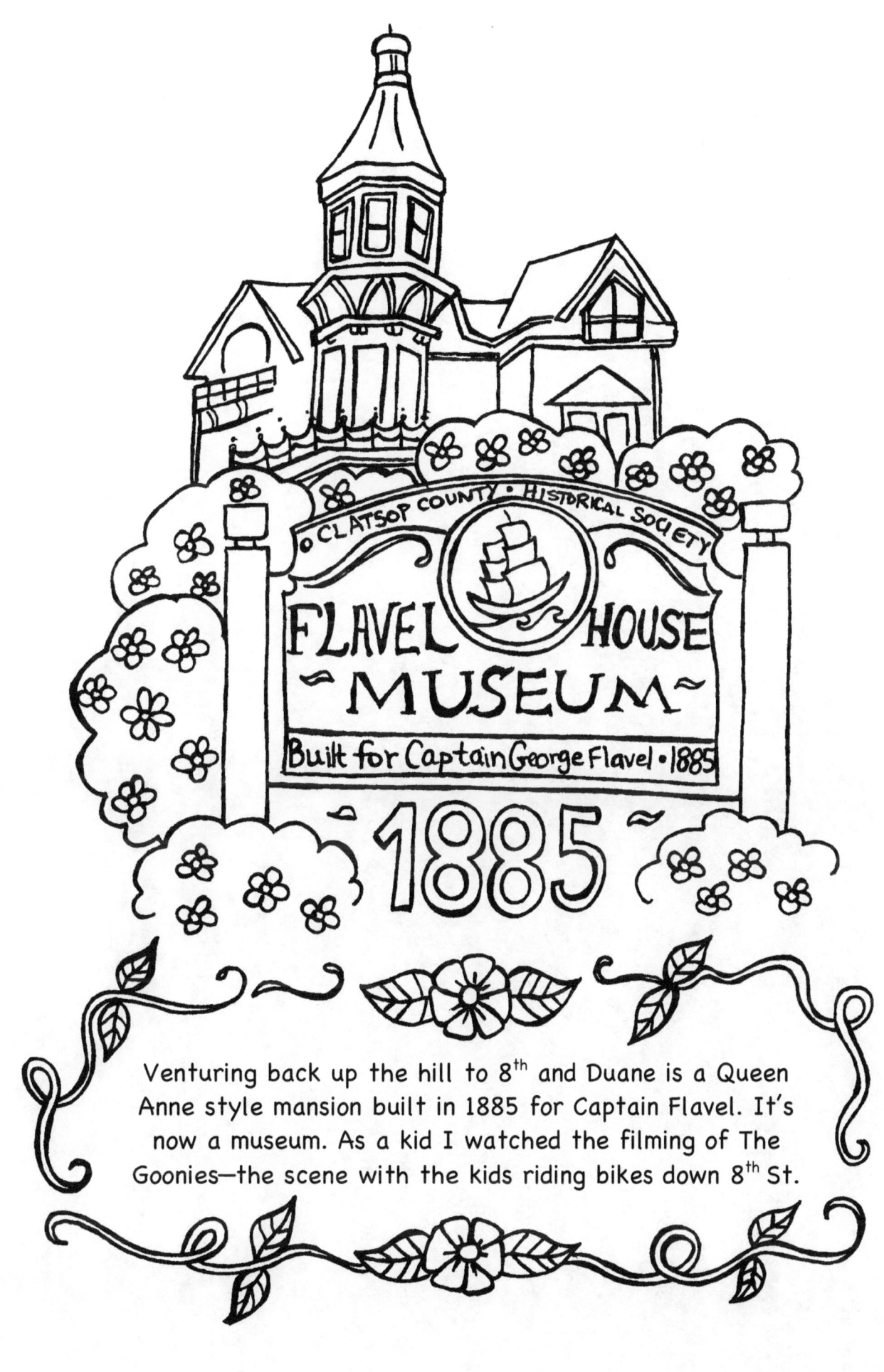

CLATSOP COUNTY · HISTORICAL SOCIETY

FLAVEL HOUSE
~MUSEUM~
Built for Captain George Flavel · 1885

~1885~

Venturing back up the hill to 8th and Duane is a Queen Anne style mansion built in 1885 for Captain Flavel. It's now a museum. As a kid I watched the filming of The Goonies—the scene with the kids riding bikes down 8th St.

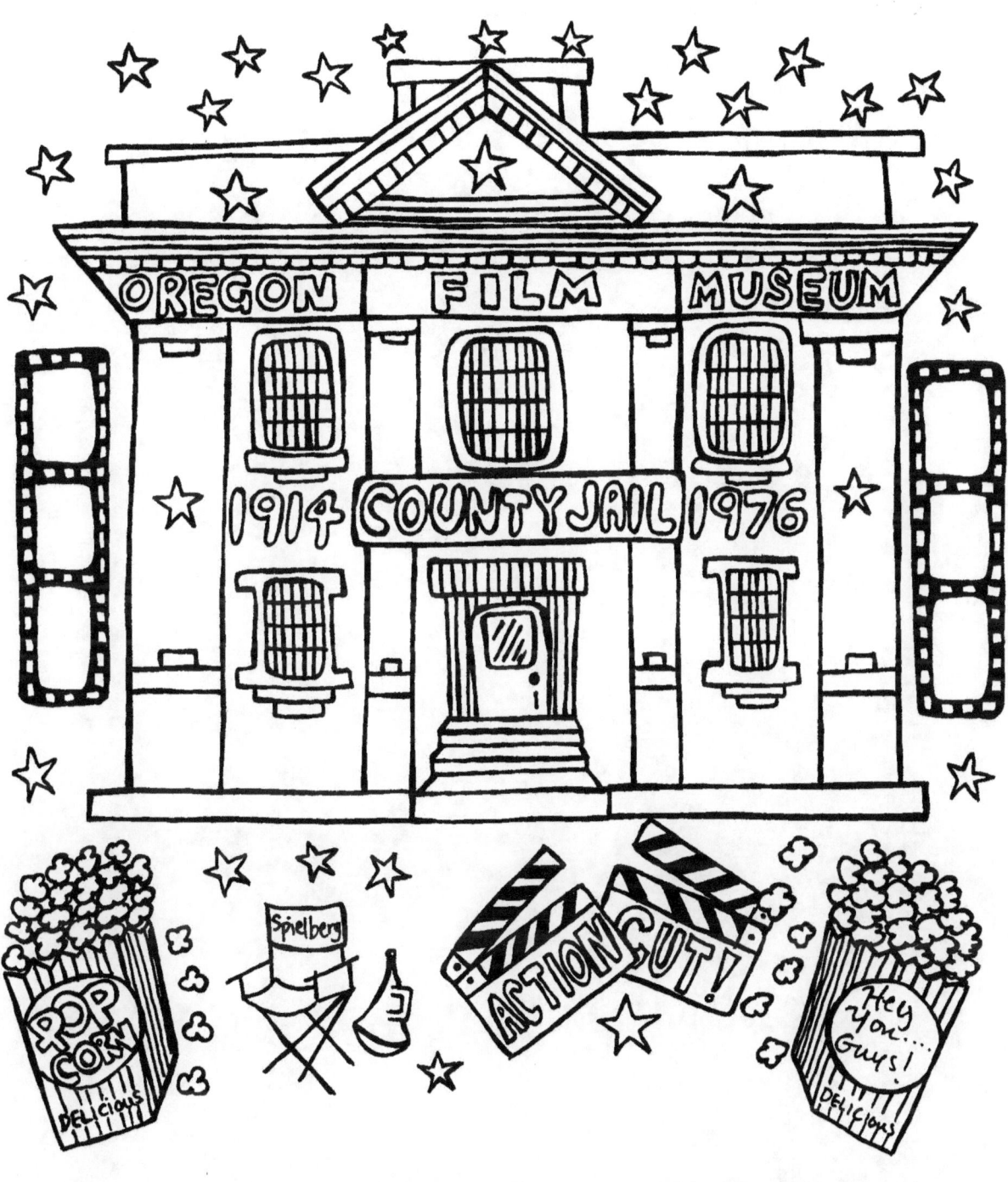

Next door to the Flavel House is The Oregon Film Museum. Inside the historic Clatsop County Jail (featured in The Goonies), you can explore movies made in Astoria. The museum aims to preserve the history of films made in Astoria, and Oregon as well.

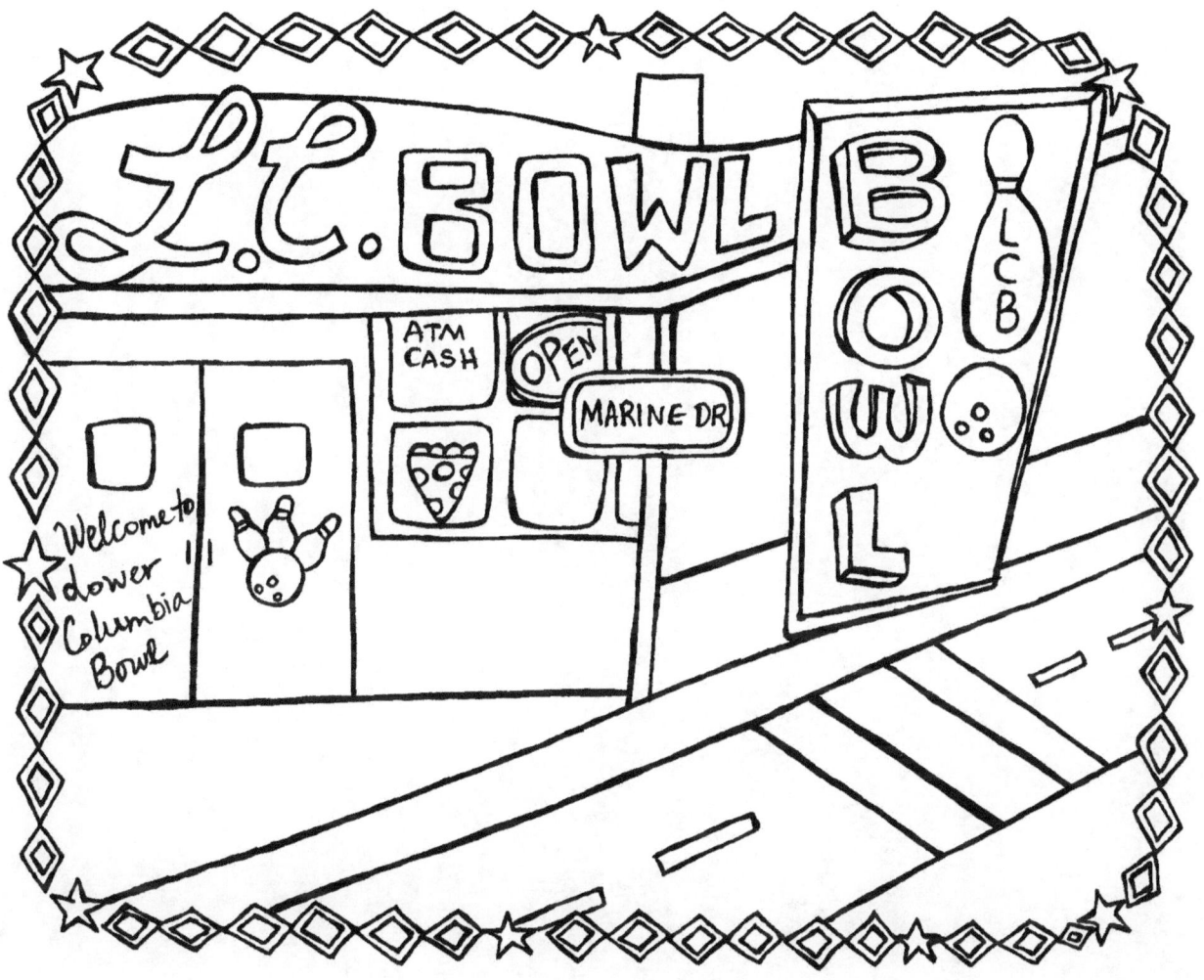

Heading back towards the River Walk, The Lower Columbia Bowl at 826 Marine Drive is home to another unforgettable Goonies moment when Chunk smashes his milkshake and pizza on the window while watching the car chase.

Goonies aside, it's still a great family place and was one of the few activities for kids growing up in Astoria.

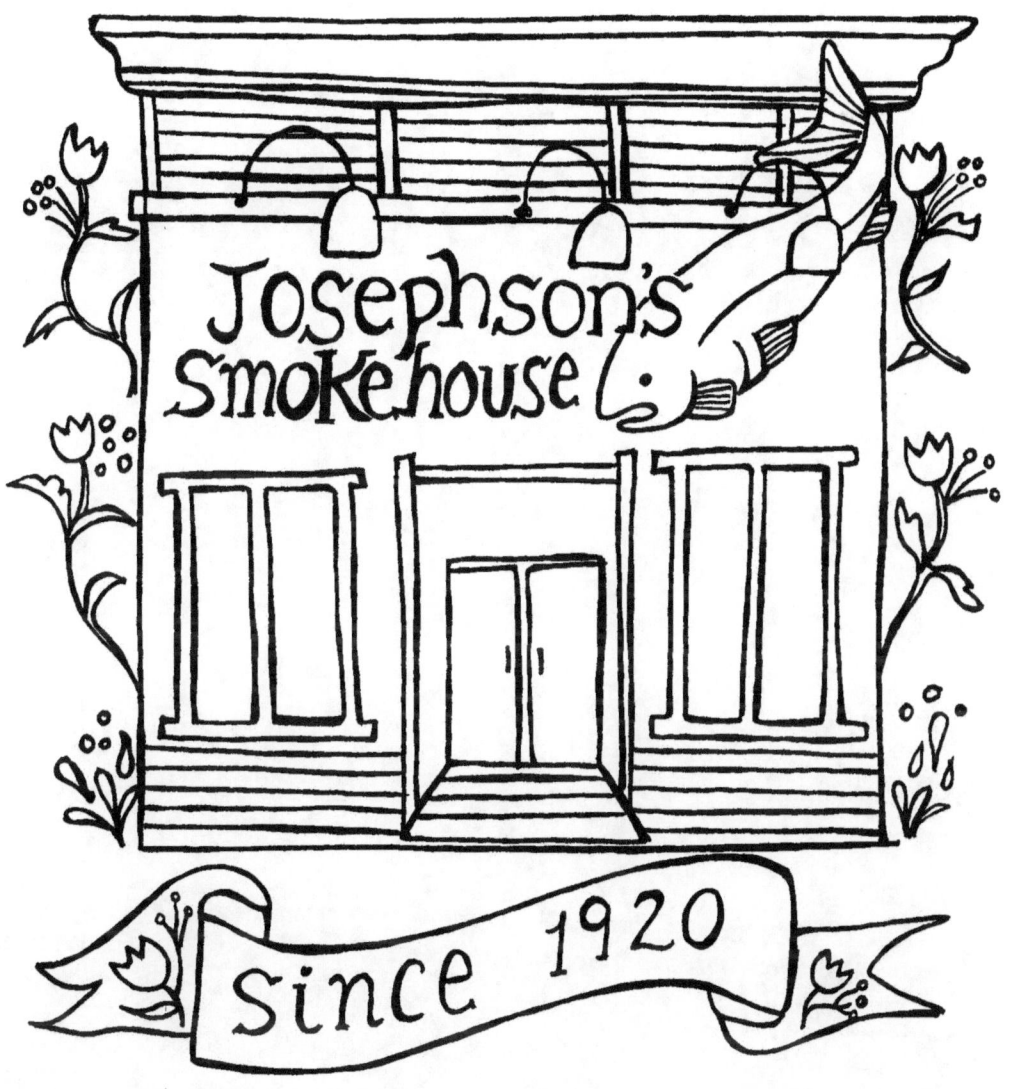

Josephson's Smoke House at 106 Marine Drive has been family owned and operated for over 90 years by a local family of commercial fishermen, fish processors and fish buyers.

They produce an authentic product, with wonderful smoked fish and other delicacies in many varieties.

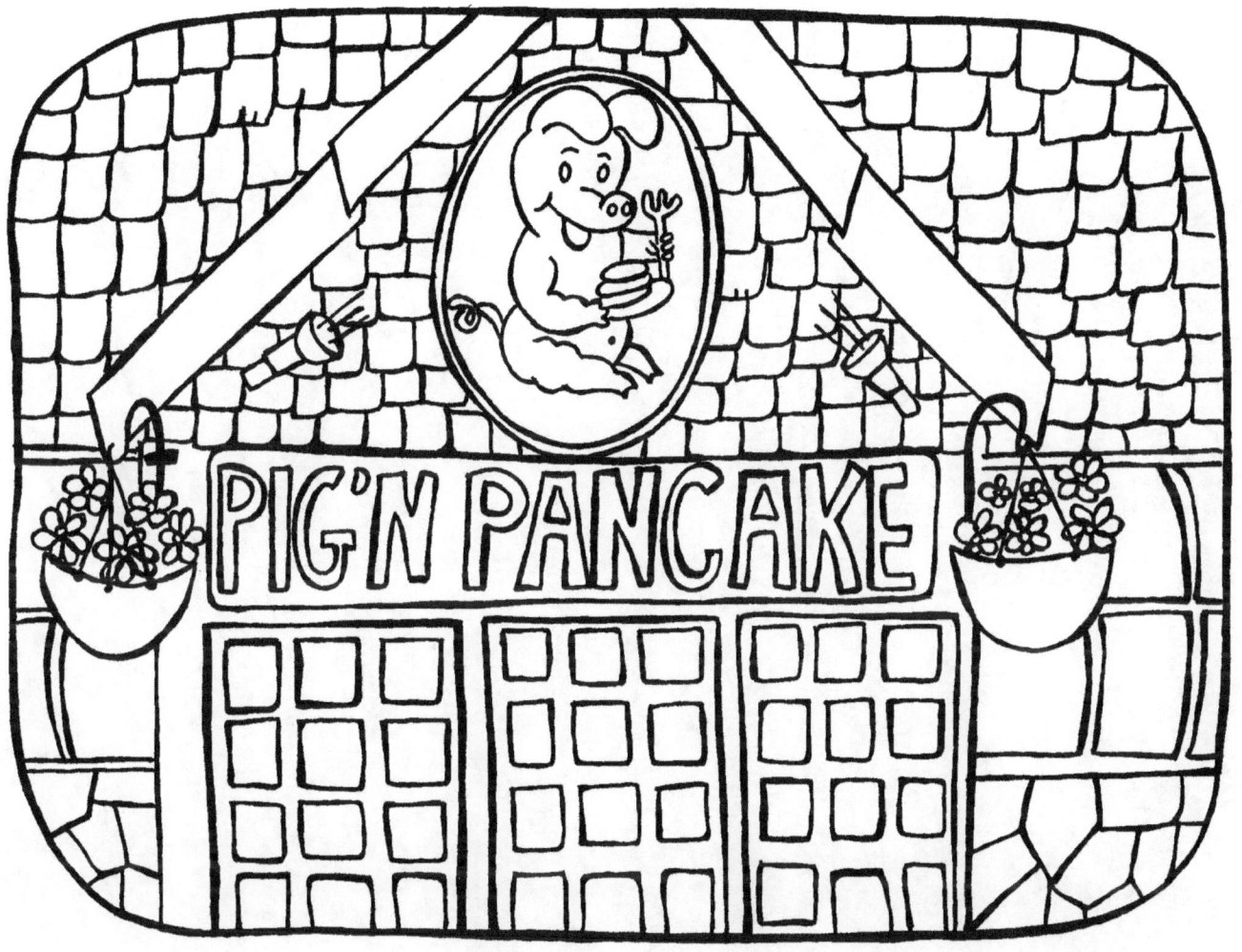

"Meet me at the Pig." It's a phrase you'll probably hear if you live in Astoria long enough. This local family dining pit stop is located at 146 West Bond and is popular for a Sunday morning breakfast or a coffee and pie up at the bar. As a kid, I have fond memories of marionberry syrup and pigs in a blanket.

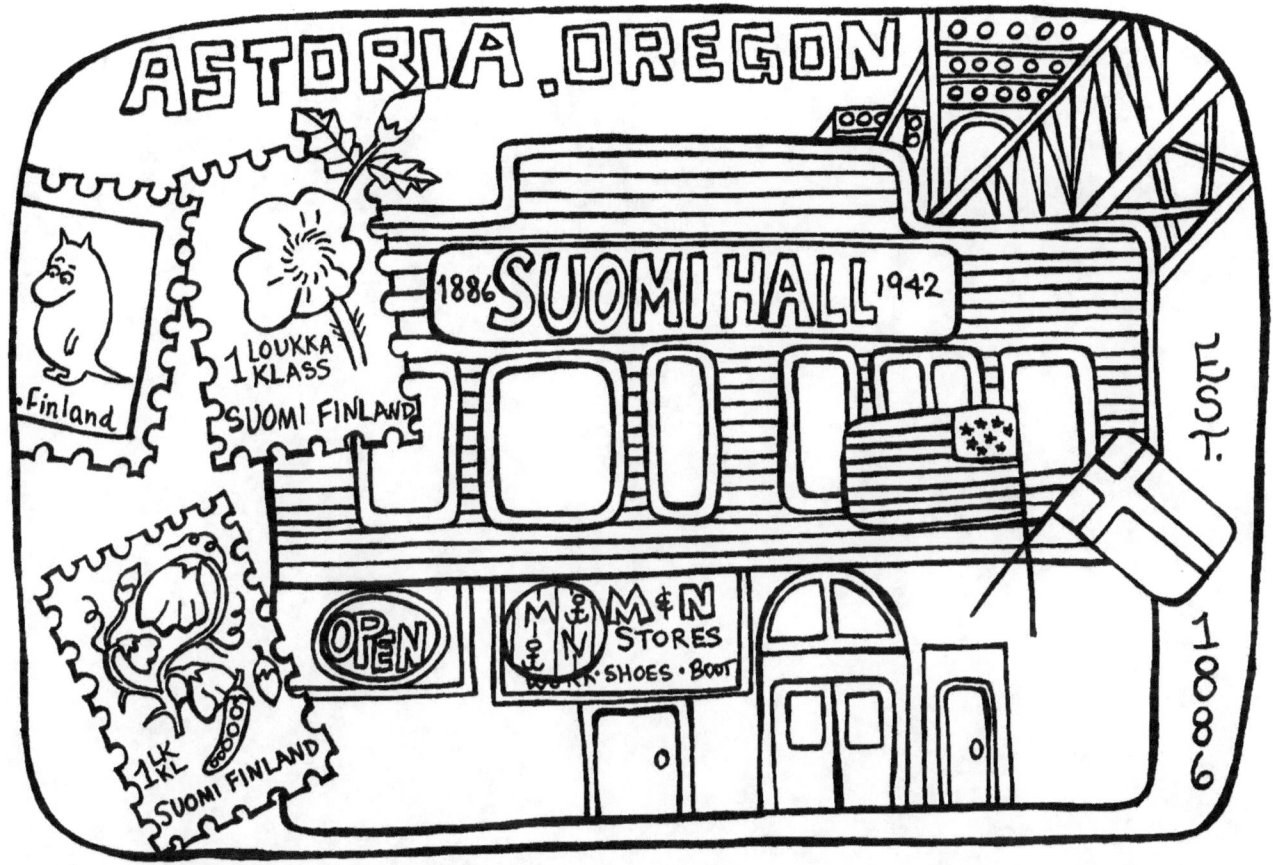

Suomi Hall is not an exclusive club only for old Finnish men. No, it's actually the United Finnish Kavala Brothers and Sisters Astoria Lodge #2 and they preserve Finnish Heritage.

The building is 131 years old. They welcome everyone to the Laksloda and Lutefisk annual dinners.

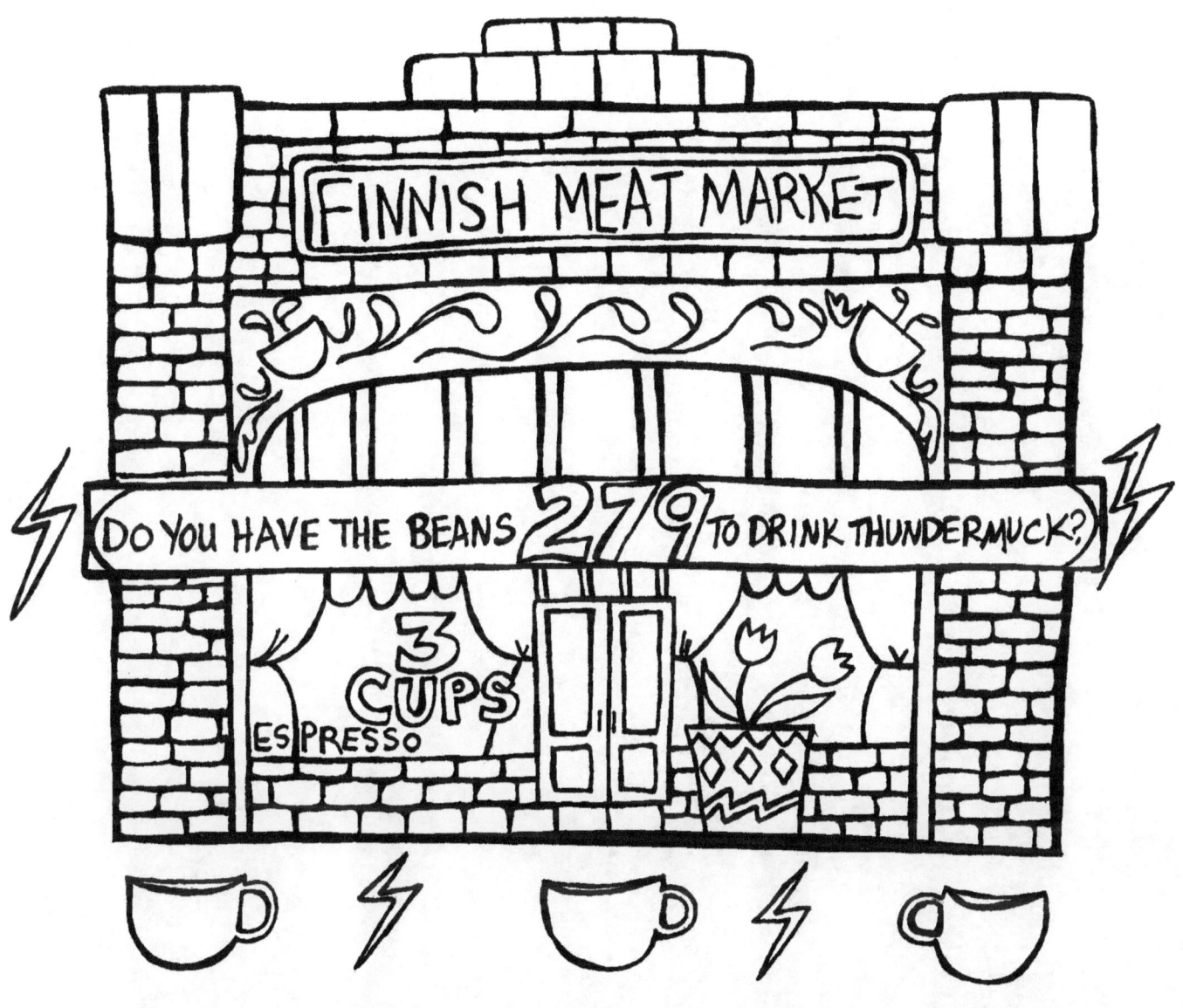

The Historic Finnish Meat Market harkens back to the Finnish presence in Uniontown. This building is home to 3 Cups Coffee Shop as well as a coffee roaster.

Located at 279 W. Marine Drive,
the nice comfy couches and the staff always makes everyone feel at home.

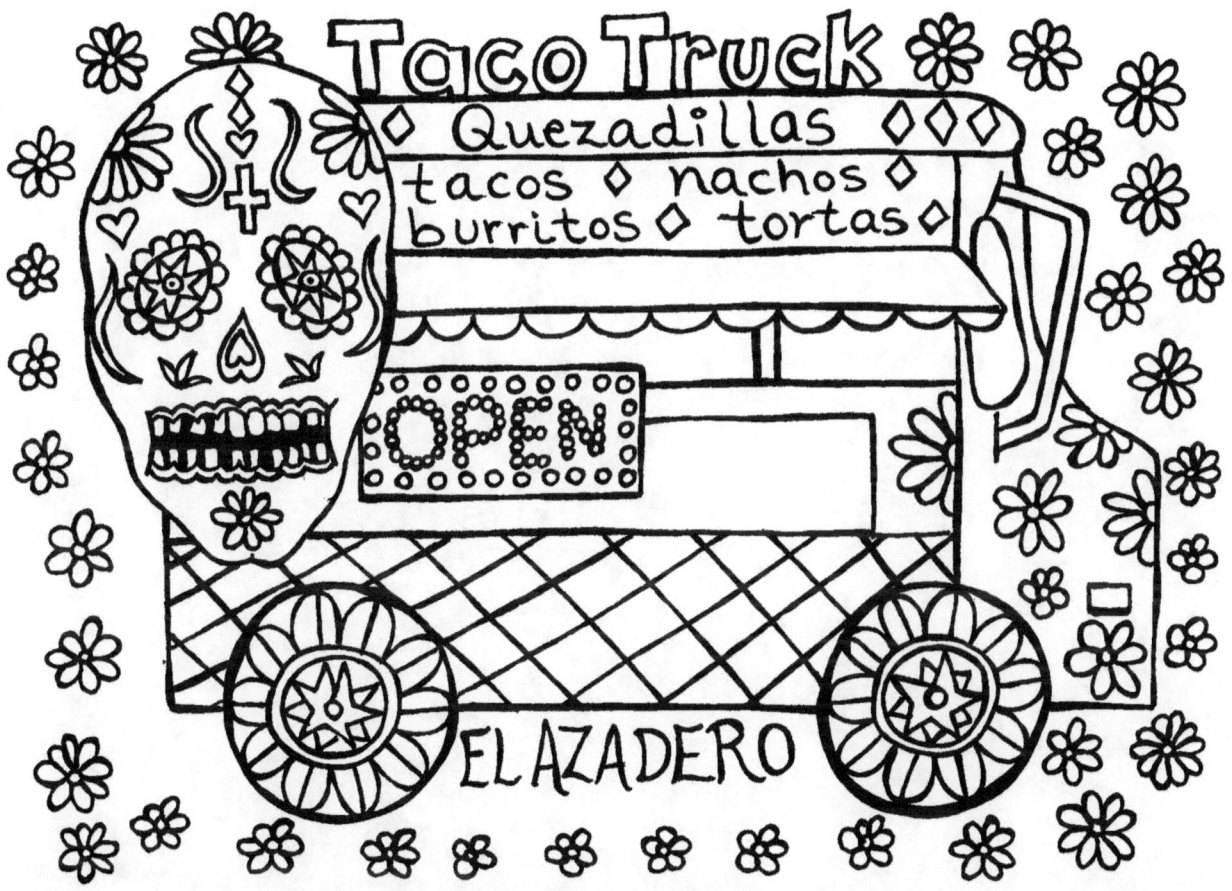

We end our East to West coloring journey at El Azadero,
a taco truck run by the Vermudez family.
It's not summer without a stop for tacos on the way to a
beach bonfire with my friends.

Until next time, hope you enjoyed My Astoria.

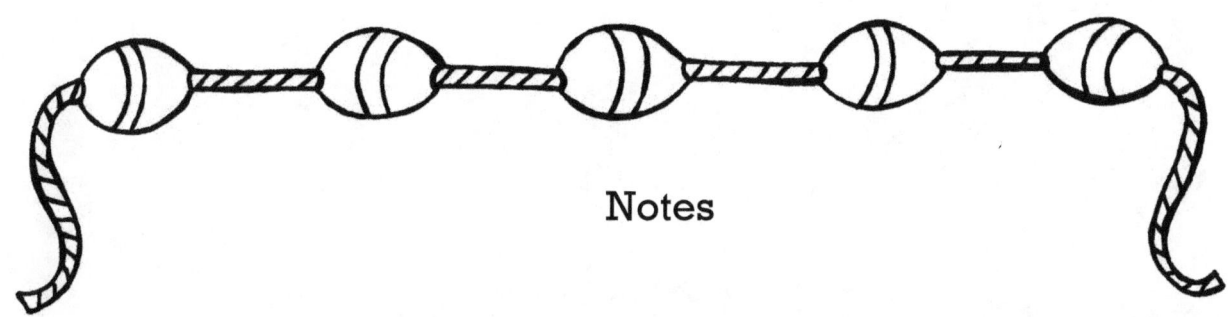

Notes

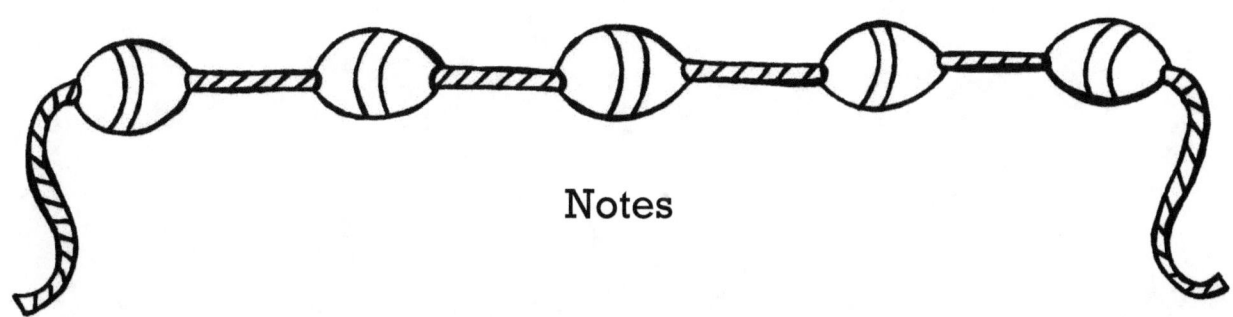

Notes

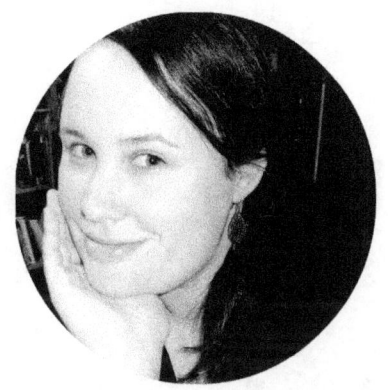

Heather Douglas is a
freelance illustrator,
writer and educator.

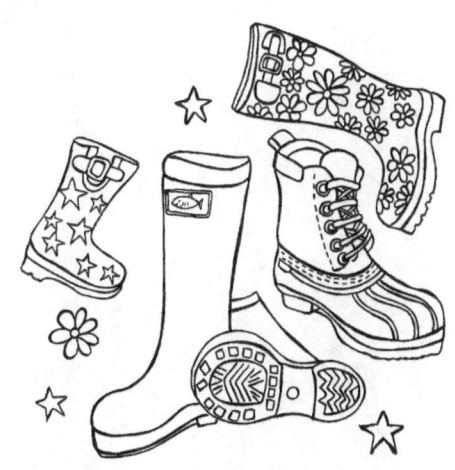

Born and raised in
Astoria, Oregon
she feels most at peace
in the forest and
enjoys a perfectly made
chai latte.

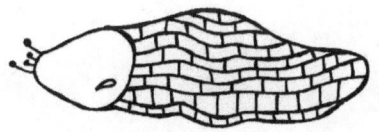

www.ingramcontent.com/pod-product-compliance
Lightning Source LLC
Chambersburg PA
CBHW080629190526
45169CB00009B/3332